How To Attract Men Diary

Brought to You by

Emmie Martins

Copyright 2015

Agenda DATE _____

TIME	DESCRIPTION

Phone Numbers

To-Do

Notes

Agenda DATE _____

TIME	DESCRIPTION

Phone Numbers

To-Do

Notes

Agenda DATE _____

TIME	DESCRIPTION

Phone Numbers

To-Do

Notes

Agenda DATE _____

TIME	DESCRIPTION

Phone Numbers

To-Do

Notes

Agenda DATE _____

TIME	DESCRIPTION

Phone Numbers

To-Do

Notes

Agenda   DATE _____

TIME	DESCRIPTION

Phone Numbers

To-Do

Notes

Agenda DATE _____

TIME	DESCRIPTION

Phone Numbers

To-Do

Notes

Agenda DATE _____

TIME	DESCRIPTION

Phone Numbers

To-Do

Notes

Agenda DATE _____

TIME	DESCRIPTION

Phone Numbers

To-Do

Notes

Agenda DATE _____

TIME	DESCRIPTION

Phone Numbers

To-Do

Notes

Agenda DATE _____

TIME	DESCRIPTION

Phone Numbers

To-Do

Notes

Agenda DATE _____

TIME	DESCRIPTION

Phone Numbers

To-Do

Notes

Agenda DATE _____

TIME | DESCRIPTION

Phone Numbers

To-Do

Notes

Agenda DATE _____

TIME	DESCRIPTION

Phone Numbers

To-Do

Notes

Agenda DATE _____

TIME | DESCRIPTION

Phone Numbers

To-Do

Notes

Agenda DATE _____

TIME	DESCRIPTION

Phone Numbers

To-Do

Notes

Agenda DATE _____

TIME | DESCRIPTION

Phone Numbers

To-Do

Notes

Agenda DATE _____

TIME	DESCRIPTION

Phone Numbers

To-Do

Notes

Agenda DATE _____

TIME	DESCRIPTION

Phone Numbers

To-Do

Notes

Agenda DATE _____

TIME	DESCRIPTION

Phone Numbers

To-Do

Notes

Agenda DATE _____

TIME	DESCRIPTION
_____	_____
_____	_____
_____	_____
_____	_____
_____	_____
_____	_____
_____	_____
_____	_____
_____	_____
_____	_____
_____	_____
_____	_____
_____	_____
_____	_____
_____	_____
_____	_____
_____	_____
_____	_____
_____	_____
_____	_____
_____	_____
_____	_____
_____	_____
_____	_____
_____	_____
_____	_____

Phone Numbers

To-Do

Notes

Agenda DATE _____

TIME	DESCRIPTION

Phone Numbers

To-Do

Notes

Agenda DATE _____

TIME	DESCRIPTION

Phone Numbers

To-Do

Notes

Agenda DATE _____

TIME	DESCRIPTION

Phone Numbers

To-Do

Notes

Agenda DATE _____

TIME	DESCRIPTION

Phone Numbers

To-Do

Notes

Agenda DATE _____

TIME	DESCRIPTION

Phone Numbers

To-Do

Notes

Agenda DATE _____

TIME	DESCRIPTION

Phone Numbers

To-Do

Notes

Agenda DATE _____

TIME | DESCRIPTION

Phone Numbers

To-Do

Notes

Agenda DATE _____

TIME	DESCRIPTION

Phone Numbers

To-Do

Notes

Agenda DATE _____

TIME	DESCRIPTION

Phone Numbers

To-Do

Notes

Agenda DATE _____

TIME	DESCRIPTION

Phone Numbers

To-Do

Notes

Agenda DATE _____

TIME	DESCRIPTION

Phone Numbers

To-Do

Notes

Agenda DATE _____

TIME	DESCRIPTION

Phone Numbers

To-Do

Notes

Agenda DATE _____

TIME	DESCRIPTION

Phone Numbers

To-Do

Notes

Agenda DATE _____

TIME	DESCRIPTION

Phone Numbers

To-Do

Notes

Agenda DATE _____

TIME	DESCRIPTION

Phone Numbers

To-Do

Notes

Agenda DATE _____

TIME	DESCRIPTION

Phone Numbers

To-Do

Notes

Agenda DATE _____

TIME	DESCRIPTION

Phone Numbers

To-Do

Notes

Agenda DATE _____

TIME	DESCRIPTION

Phone Numbers

To-Do

Notes

Agenda DATE _____

TIME	DESCRIPTION

Phone Numbers

To-Do

Notes

Agenda DATE _____

TIME	DESCRIPTION

Phone Numbers

To-Do

Notes

Agenda DATE _____

TIME	DESCRIPTION

Phone Numbers

To-Do

Notes

Agenda DATE _____

TIME	DESCRIPTION

Phone Numbers

To-Do

Notes

Agenda DATE _____

TIME	DESCRIPTION

Phone Numbers

To-Do

Notes

Agenda DATE _____

TIME	DESCRIPTION

Phone Numbers

To-Do

Notes

Agenda DATE _____

TIME	DESCRIPTION

Phone Numbers

To-Do

Notes

Agenda DATE _____

TIME	DESCRIPTION

Phone Numbers

To-Do

Notes

Agenda DATE _____

TIME	DESCRIPTION

Phone Numbers

To-Do

Notes

Agenda DATE _____

TIME	DESCRIPTION

Phone Numbers

To-Do

Notes

Agenda DATE _____

TIME	DESCRIPTION

Phone Numbers

To-Do

Notes

Agenda DATE _____

TIME	DESCRIPTION

Phone Numbers

To-Do

Notes

Agenda DATE _____

TIME	DESCRIPTION

Phone Numbers

To-Do

Notes

Agenda DATE _____

TIME	DESCRIPTION

Phone Numbers

To-Do

Notes

Agenda DATE _____

TIME	DESCRIPTION

Phone Numbers

To-Do

Notes

Agenda DATE _____

TIME	DESCRIPTION

Phone Numbers

To-Do

Notes

Agenda DATE _____

TIME	DESCRIPTION

Phone Numbers

To-Do

Notes

Agenda DATE _____

TIME	DESCRIPTION

Phone Numbers

To-Do

Notes

Agenda DATE _____

TIME	DESCRIPTION

Phone Numbers

To-Do

Notes

Agenda DATE _____

TIME	DESCRIPTION

Phone Numbers

To-Do

Notes

Agenda DATE _____

TIME	DESCRIPTION

Phone Numbers

To-Do

Notes

Agenda DATE _____

TIME	DESCRIPTION

Phone Numbers

To-Do

Notes

Agenda DATE _____

TIME | DESCRIPTION

Phone Numbers

To-Do

Notes

Agenda DATE _____

TIME	DESCRIPTION

Phone Numbers

To-Do

Notes

Agenda DATE _____

TIME	DESCRIPTION

Phone Numbers

To-Do

Notes

Agenda DATE _____

TIME	DESCRIPTION

Phone Numbers

To Do

Notes

Agenda DATE _____

TIME | DESCRIPTION

Phone Numbers

To-Do

Notes

Agenda DATE _____

TIME	DESCRIPTION

Phone Numbers

To-Do

Notes

Agenda DATE _____

TIME	DESCRIPTION

Phone Numbers

To-Do

Notes

Agenda DATE _____

TIME	DESCRIPTION

Phone Numbers

To-Do

Notes

Agenda DATE _____

TIME	DESCRIPTION

Phone Numbers

To-Do

Notes

Agenda DATE _____

TIME	DESCRIPTION

Phone Numbers

To Do

Notes

Agenda DATE _____

TIME	DESCRIPTION

Phone Numbers

To-Do

Notes

Agenda DATE _____

TIME	DESCRIPTION

Phone Numbers

To-Do

Notes

Agenda DATE _____

TIME	DESCRIPTION

Phone Numbers

To-Do

Notes

Agenda DATE _____

TIME   DESCRIPTION

Phone Numbers

To-Do

Notes

Agenda DATE _____

TIME	DESCRIPTION

Phone Numbers

To-Do

Notes

Agenda DATE _____

TIME	DESCRIPTION

Phone Numbers

To-Do

Notes

Agenda DATE _____

TIME	DESCRIPTION

Phone Numbers

To-Do

Notes

Agenda DATE _____

TIME	DESCRIPTION

Phone Numbers

To-Do

Notes

Agenda DATE _____

TIME	DESCRIPTION

Phone Numbers

To-Do

Notes

Agenda DATE _____

TIME | DESCRIPTION

Phone Numbers

To-Do

Notes

Agenda DATE _____

TIME	DESCRIPTION

Phone Numbers

To-Do

Notes

Agenda DATE _____

TIME	DESCRIPTION

Phone Numbers

To-Do

Notes

Agenda DATE _____

TIME	DESCRIPTION

Phone Numbers

To-Do

Notes

Agenda DATE _____

TIME	DESCRIPTION

Phone Numbers

To-Do

Notes

Agenda DATE _____

TIME	DESCRIPTION

Phone Numbers

To-Do

Notes

Agenda DATE _____

TIME	DESCRIPTION

Phone Numbers

To-Do

Notes

Agenda DATE _____

TIME	DESCRIPTION

Phone Numbers

To-Do

Notes

Agenda DATE _____

TIME	DESCRIPTION

Phone Numbers

To-Do

Notes

Agenda DATE _____

TIME | DESCRIPTION

Phone Numbers

To-Do

Notes

Agenda DATE _____

TIME	DESCRIPTION

Phone Numbers

To-Do

Notes

Agenda DATE _____

TIME	DESCRIPTION

Phone Numbers

To-Do

Notes

Agenda DATE _____

TIME	DESCRIPTION

Phone Numbers

To-Do

Notes

Agenda DATE _____

TIME	DESCRIPTION

Phone Numbers

To-Do

Notes

Agenda DATE _____

TIME	DESCRIPTION

Phone Numbers

To-Do

Notes

Agenda DATE _____

TIME	DESCRIPTION

Phone Numbers

To-Do

Notes

Agenda DATE _____

TIME	DESCRIPTION

Phone Numbers

To-Do

Notes

Agenda DATE _____

TIME	DESCRIPTION

Phone Numbers

To-Do

Notes

Agenda DATE _____

TIME	DESCRIPTION

Phone Numbers

To-Do

Notes

Agenda DATE _____

TIME	DESCRIPTION

Phone Numbers

To-Do

Notes

Agenda DATE _____

TIME	DESCRIPTION

Phone Numbers

To-Do

Notes

Agenda DATE _____

TIME	DESCRIPTION

Phone Numbers

To-Do

Notes

Agenda DATE _____

TIME	DESCRIPTION

Phone Numbers

To-Do

Notes

Agenda DATE _____

TIME	DESCRIPTION

Phone Numbers

To-Do

Notes

Agenda DATE _____

TIME	DESCRIPTION

Phone Numbers

To-Do

Notes

Agenda DATE _____

TIME	DESCRIPTION

Phone Numbers

To-Do

Notes

Agenda DATE _____

TIME	DESCRIPTION

Phone Numbers

To-Do

Notes

Agenda DATE _____

TIME	DESCRIPTION

Phone Numbers

To-Do

Notes

Agenda DATE _____

TIME	DESCRIPTION

Phone Numbers

To-Do

Notes

Agenda DATE _____

TIME	DESCRIPTION

Phone Numbers

To-Do

Notes

Agenda DATE _____

TIME	DESCRIPTION

Phone Numbers

To-Do

Notes

Agenda DATE _____

TIME	DESCRIPTION

Phone Numbers

To-Do

Notes

Agenda DATE _____

TIME	DESCRIPTION

Phone Numbers

To-Do

Notes

Agenda DATE _____

TIME	DESCRIPTION

Phone Numbers

To-Do

Notes

Agenda DATE _____

TIME	DESCRIPTION

Phone Numbers

To-Do

Notes

Agenda DATE _____

TIME	DESCRIPTION

Phone Numbers

To-Do

Notes

Agenda DATE _____

TIME	DESCRIPTION

Phone Numbers

To-Do

Notes

Agenda DATE _____

TIME	DESCRIPTION

Phone Numbers

To-Do

Notes

Agenda DATE _____

TIME | DESCRIPTION

Phone Numbers

To-Do

Notes

Agenda DATE _____

TIME	DESCRIPTION

Phone Numbers

To-Do

Notes

www.ingramcontent.com/pod-product-compliance
Lightning Source LLC
Chambersburg PA
CBHW080811040426
42333CB00062B/2684